reborn buildings

Author: Arian Mostaedi
Publishers: Carles Broto & Josep Mª Minguet
Graphic Design: Judith Roig
Layout Design: Albert Valero, Héctor Navarro
Production: Francisco Orduña
Architectural Adviser: Pilar Chueca
Texts: María Ribas, Jacobo Krauel
Proofreading: Monika Camacho

© Carles Broto i Comerma (English edition)
Ausias Marc, 20. 4-2
08010 Barcelona, Spain
Tel.: +34 93 301 21 99 Fax: +34 93 301 00 21
www.linksbooks.net
info@linksbooks.net

Printed in Barcelona, Spain

reborn buildings

index

Introduction

8   **Terver, Couvert & Beddock**
Villa Schumann–Sizaret

18   **Fisher & Friedman Associates**
The Oriental Warehouse

26   **Luigi Ferrario**
Home Studio for a Graphic Designer

36   **Giovanni Scheibler**
Loft conversion in Zurich

46   **Kalhöfer & Korschildgen**
Holiday House in Normandy

54   **Jordi Borras & Carmen Padrosa**
Vivienda a Castelló d'Empúries

64   **Ottorino Berselli & Cecilia Cassina**
Ristrutturazione in Manerbio

74   **Daniele Marques & Bruno Zurkirchen**
Haus in Bergün

84   **Oswald Mathias Ungers**
Wasserturm

92   **Delogu, Lixi, Constantini & Andreeva**
Borgo di Sacrofano

102   **José Paulo Dos Santos**
Pousada en el Convento Dos Loios

110   **Louis Kloster**
Sola Ruin Church

116   **Michael Graves**
Graves Residence: The Warehouse

124   **Claudio Lazzarini & Carl Pickering**
Residence on Sicilian Coast

134   **Alois Peitz**
St. Maximin Sportliches und Kulturelles Zentrum

144   **Sergio Calatroni**
Casa Galería Uchida

152   **Julia B. Bolles & Peter L. Wilson**
Haus Dub

160   **Mathias Klotz & Felipe Assadi**
Hotel Terrantai

170   **Stan Bolt**
O'Sullivan House

introduction

Rehabilitating architecture involves delving into the past in order to rewrite history and give it new life. To restore, to preserve, to repair, to reconstruct, to interven, etc., this ambiguous family of terms refers to the same controversial practise that seeks to refurbish old spaces in order to give them a new use, whilst safeguarding their historical character and holding back excessive expressions of genius and personality by the designer. It is a difficult balance involving many conflicts over historical research and technical solutions, in which the architect often comes out as the loser. The harshest critics tend to pick out unequivocally new gestures, the more personal marks of identity, the elements that the pro-fessional has distributed throughout the work in order to highlight the dialogue between the freshness of the new language and the majestic character of the venerable building.

The projects that are presented here cover a wide range of situations that range from the restoration of an old convent to house a modern hotel to the adaptation of a Gothic church for such an unlikely use as sports centre.

Curiously, many of these works were created to meet needs of an ecclesiastic type: though these pages include many works of old places, villas and castles, there are many conversions of monasteries, churches and convents. Their original spaces, full of suggestions, now accept a new and undoubtedly more profane life.

Guillaume TERVER, Fabienne COUVERT & Xavier BEDDOCK

Villa SCHUMANN-SIZARET
(Chevanny, France)

In this restructuring and conversion of an agricultural building into a dwelling, for the perusal of the framework and for financial reasons the architects wished to develop a sequential project in three phases that would successively occupy the three arches of the building.

The house (in dressed stonework) is composed of three parts, each housing different functions. The first arch contains the Winter House, isolated, heated and with all the prime necessities. The second one is for intermediate activities, interior and external functions of spring-autumn, with a veranda and an internal garden.

The third arch was designed to house—later—the Summer House, with supplementary bedrooms.

The existing materials such as the stone of the window breast and the wood lintels were respected. The internal intervention in the first phase consists of the creation of two technical wood boxes, one per level, housing all the building's functional requirements (cooking, toilet, storage, heating, etc.). These boxes occupy a central position, which permits the use of their four sides and allows a corresponding future subdivision of the initial internal volume free from the basic functional constraints.

The entry, in the central arch, is marked by a protruding wood module that allows an integration and an interaction with the garden and the surrounding orchard. The natural lighting of this bay is achieved thanks to the use of glass tiles on the roofing in the form of an opus incertum. The third arch will be carried out at a later stage.

PHOTOGRAPHS: T. DELHASTE

Site plan

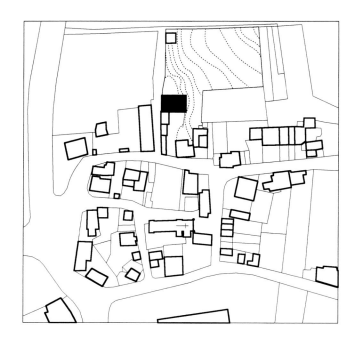

Axonometric view

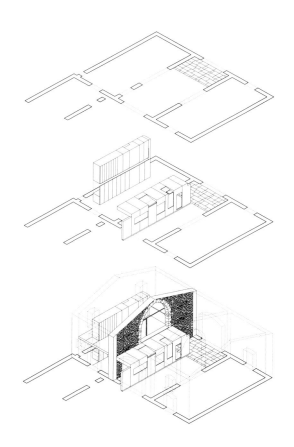

The entrance located under the central arch is marked by a protruding module of okumé wood, allowing the integration of the dwelling with the garden and the nearby orchard.

Upper floor plan

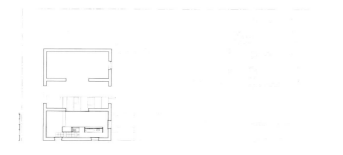

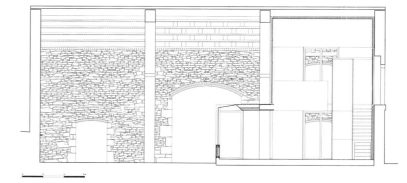

Lower floor plan

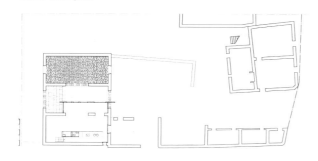

As can be seen in this page, some of the roof tiles have been replaced by glass tiles in order to allow light to penetrate the interior.

The project consists of the rehabilitation of an agricultural building for conversion into a dwelling. This will be carried out in three phases that will successively occupy the three bays into which the barn is divided.

The first phase of the project consists of the creation of two blocks of wood and glass that house the basic functions of a dwelling. These blocks have been located in a central position to allow the exploration of their four sides and the free distribution of the interior space.

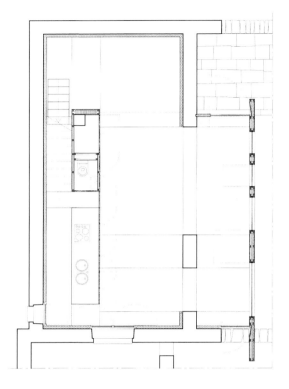

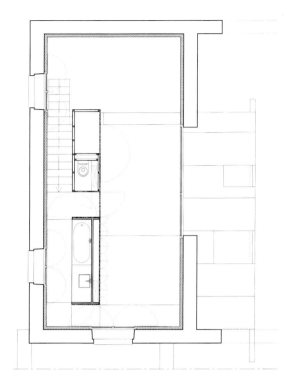

On this page, views of the kitchen and the living-dining room located on the ground floor. The kitchen, located under the staircase leading to the upper floor, takes advantage of the fact that the steps do not have a riser thus facilitating natural lighting.

FISHER & FRIEDMAN *Associates*

The Oriental WAREHOUSE
(San Francisco, USA)

The Oriental Warehouse constructed in 1868 on the San Francisco waterfront was converted to 66 live/work lofts. It is divided into three equal bays of which the outer two were damaged by fire and earthquake. The surviving parts of the north and west walls have been incorporated into the design. New light courts were inserted into each of the three structural bays. Facing them, new steel frame structures contain the residential spaces.

The new construction is set back from the existing walls in order to showcase them and allow light into the residential units. Since the building was a bonded warehouse, there were no windows in the exterior walls, and preservation groups were consulted to agree a proposal that would allow additional light into the courts.

At the middle bay, the 19th-century timber construction was reclaimed and adapted to the new design. New 21st-century steel warehouse structures were inserted into the remains of the damaged outside bays. The new facades that face the light courts in all three bays are clad in industrial corrugated metal and all windows are aluminium sash. Within the height of the existing walls in all three bays the architects designed two stacked two-storey lofts spaces, all of which face onto the three light courts. The two garages are placed partially underground in the north and south bays. All three bays are linked at the front by a new four-storey lobby. Access to the living units is from the lobby into the light courts through exterior entry patios, and into the lower units.

PHOTOGRAPHS: CHARLES CALLISTER

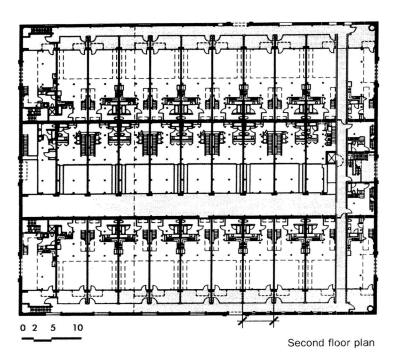

Second floor plan

On this double page, several external views of the scheme from dif-ferent angles, showing the tense relationship that is established between the new pro-posal and the existing architecture.

The architects have kept intact what was left of the original external structure of exposed masonry.

It was first stabilised and then the 66 new apartments clad with metal panels, distributed in three rows along the building, were inserted in the interior.

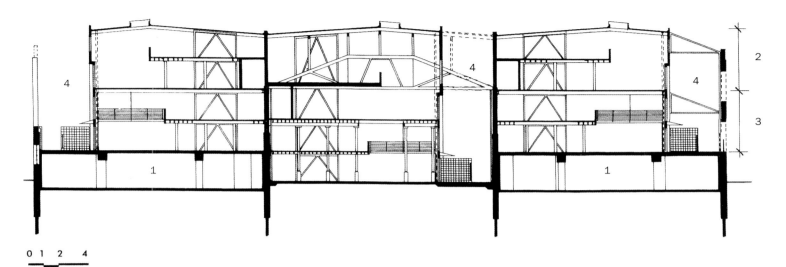

0 1 2 4

On the facade, where the old meets the new, the glass and the structure of galvanized metal are set against the exposed masonry walls that have been conserved, creating a dynamic tension between the new proposal and the existing elements.

North-south section

1. Garage
2. Upper floor plan
3. Lower floor plan
4. Light Court

The dwellings, inserted in a space that suggests a provisional and temporary character, are a functional adaptation of an old industrial structure. In the interior, the inhabitants cohabit naturally with ventilation conduits, beams, columns, metal joists, exposed masonry walls and wooden surfaces.

Luigi FERRARIO

Home Studio
FOR A GRAPHIC DESIGNER
(Bergamo, Italy)

A space with an unusual arrangement, in a traditional ancient Lombardian three-storey house represents the place in which Luigi Ferrario experiments, through a rarefied language, his own vocation to dialogue with old, sedimented forms and materials.

The architectural shell is characterised by a vertical volume of merely seven square meters, used for the bathroom, the staircase, the kitchen below and the sofabed in front of the fireplace, connected above to a work area distributed horizontally with respect to the house.

The transformation of the available space has been achieved without disrupting the characteristics of the original structure: the vault, the floor above it in terracotta with inclined steps, and the stone masonry.

The introduction of an original structure in iron, glass and wood succeeds in modifying the space and connecting the two floors: through studied additions and minimal subtractions (demolitions) it has been possible to provide for all the functions necessary for domestic life without having to subdivide the available space to obtain space for the indispensable kitchen and bathroom. A light, spiralling staircase with steps in metal web leads to an area with terracota floor and then the studio area dominated by the surfaces in light wood of the attic and the floor. The combination of natural materials, or materials that have been "naturalised" through measured transparencies, such as beech, teak, glass, grids in galvanised iron and structural elements, along with a sophisticated research of the arrangement of the facilities has guaranteed a felicitous co-existence and superimposition of new and ancient parts where the new is enhanced without mortifying the original structure.

PHOTOGRAPHS: ALBERTO PIOVANO

Through a careful intervention involving minimum demolition work, a new steel, glass and wood structure transforms the interior space and connects the two floors.

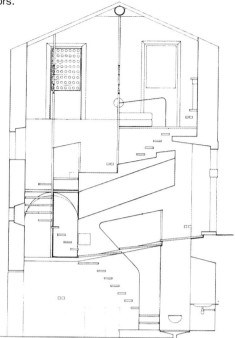

Axonometric view

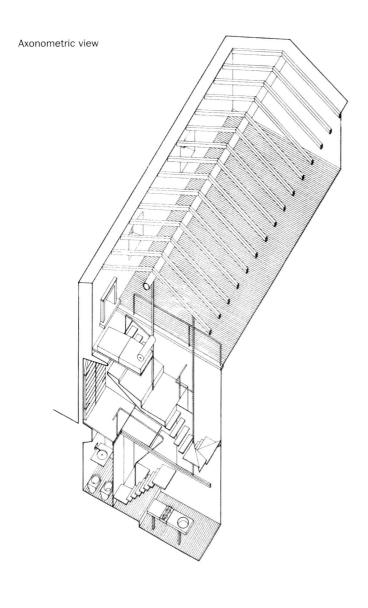

Second floor plan

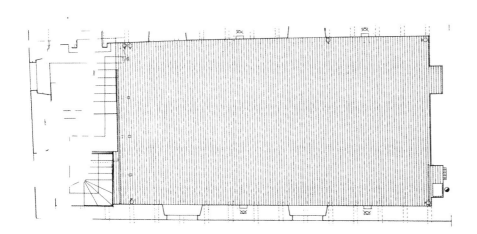

The bathroom and the small kitchen located on the ground floor are organised to avoid excessive subdivision of the space. As can be seen in the photograph above, the bathroom has a satin-finish sliding glass door.

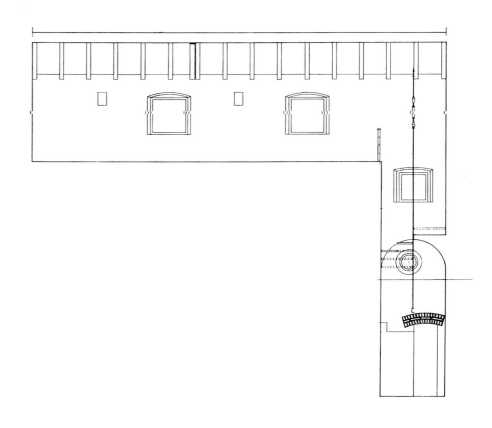

Views of the staircase to the upper floor. Its structure is characterised by the conservation of the vaults that cover it and the original terracotta floor.

On the right-hand page, views of the study. This is bounded by two wooden planes of a light colour (the floor and sloping roof), masonry walls and rendered, white-painted surfaces.

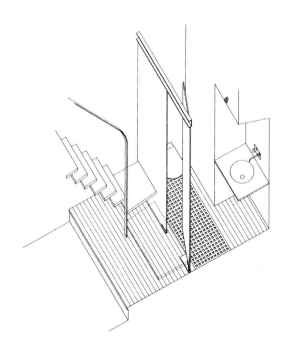

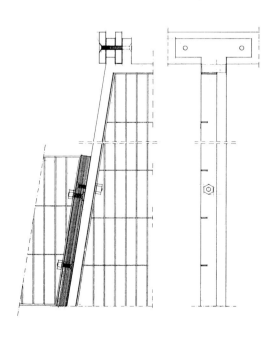

Giovanni SCHEIBLER

Loft CONVERSION IN ZURICH
(Zürich, Switzerland)

In converting the loft space in this house the aim was to create extra living space and to bring more light into the top floor flat, while respecting the characteristic turn-of-the-century outward appearance of the building. Ecological and economic factors also had a role to play. The architects created a central hall, lit from above by a new rooflight set in the ridge of the mansard roof, 7m above the hall floor, There are no fittings that block the path of light even the gallery floor is of clear glass. Light can also filter through translucent walls into the rooms bordering the hall. Sliding partition elements further help to create space and versatility, in contrast to the usual narrow confines of such flats. The materials used for the new hall are clearly legible against the existing building structure. Anthracite-coloured metal, chrome steel and glass stand next to plaster walls and wood. The fine lines of the elements of the hall complement the theme of transparency. The girders supporting the gallery are pairs of tensioned RHS-sections, resting on brackets on the mansard structure.

The cable bracing eliminates any vibrations along the slim sections. The safety glass flooring sheets rest on a double layer of rubber to reduce noise. Chrome steel is used for the hand rail and the horizontal cabling. The frame of the sliding partitions is of narrow square tube sections. Between the glazing layers is white glass lining welded to the panes at the side.

PHOTOGRAPHS: ALEX SPICHALE

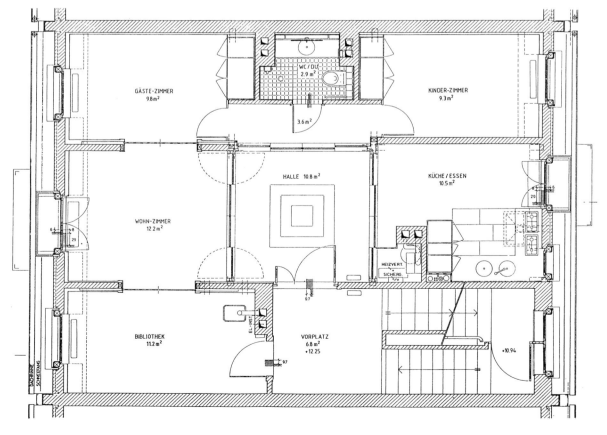

GÄSTE-ZIMMER
9.8 m²

WC / DU
2.9 m²

KINDER-ZIMMER
9.3 m²

3.6 m²

HALLE 10.8 m²

KÜCHE / ESSEN
10.5 m²

WOHN-ZIMMER
12.2 m²

HEIZVERT.
+
SICHERG.

BIBLIOTHEK
11.2 m²

EL-INST.

VORPLATZ
6.8 m²
+ 12.25

+10.94

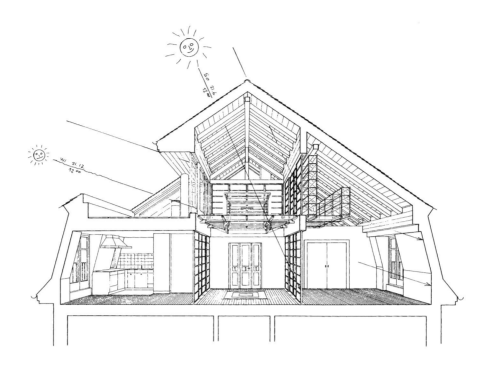

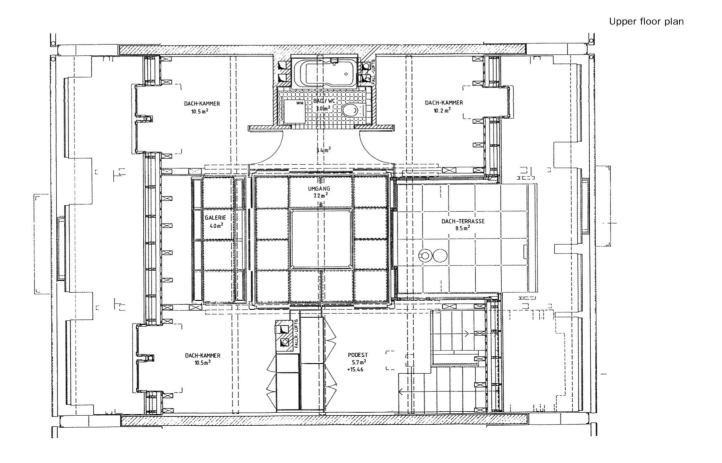

The dwelling is organized around a central hall that is top-lit by a skylight.
The light comes through the translucent glass panels into the rooms surrounding the central hall.

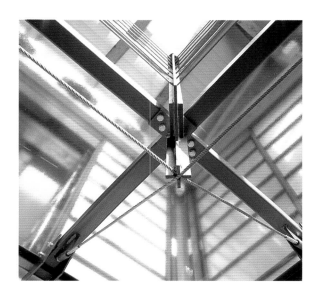

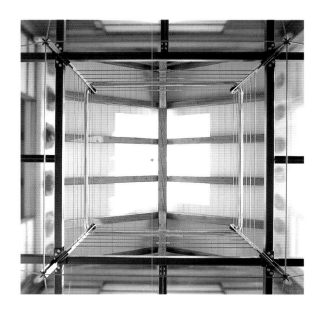

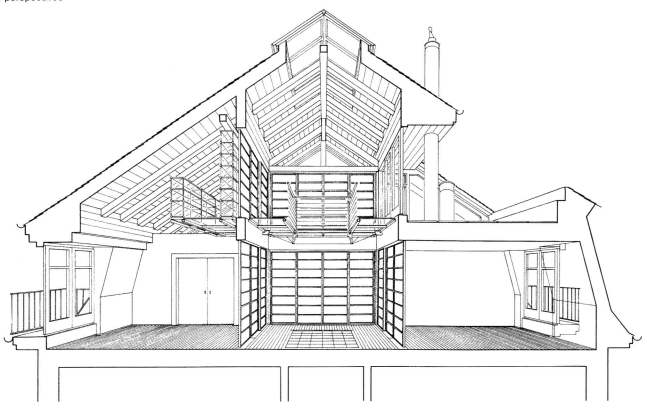

The materials used to build the central hall (steel and glass) are easily recognisable, contrasting with the existing structure of the building.

Section through the kitchen

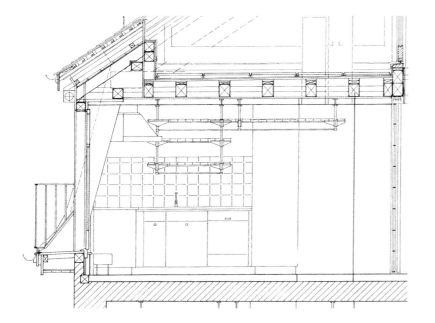

The kitchen, reached directly through the central hall, has been completely redesigned to create two sharply differentiated spaces within it: the work area and a small eating area.

Interior elevations

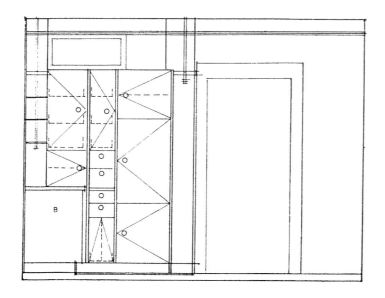

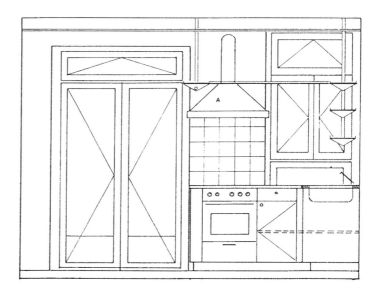

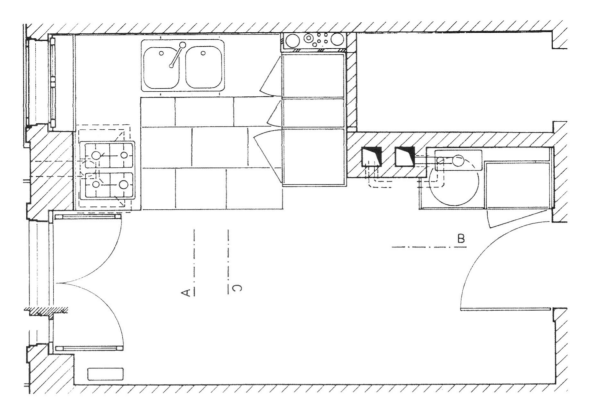

In the kitchen, a system of stainless steel suspended shelves provide visual organization of the space.

KALHÖFER &
KORSCHILDGEN

Holiday House IN NORMANDY
(Normandy, France)

The old Norman farmhouse was in extremely condition before the conversion. The aim of the design was to let the holiday house appear as an original building rather than a museum-piece. The most urgent building measures for the conversion of the building were the reconstruction of the existing structure and the fitting out of the kitchen and bathroom. Matching the often collage-like structure of development in the nearby environment, the concept provides for two distinct parts by complementing the historical building with a separate modern building. The layout, light, material and colour should provide the inhabitant with a different living experience in the new building and in the traditionally restored old building.

The existing building was reconstructed removing the defective elements and using any old materials that could be conserved.

The oak doors, wooden floors, natural stone walls and chimneys were reconstructed by the architects according to traditional regional details.

The new building concentrates the necessary technical facilities of a house at a few points. A steel framework serves as a supporting grid for the sanitary fittings and a kind of picture plane to which the coloured surfaces of the finishings are fixed. Flowing transitions of the structure from inside to outside help to create a holiday home that can be used in different ways, depending on the season. The boundaries between inner and outer space are translucent and fluid thanks to the generous use of glass, which is specially striking during the lighting of the individual functional units at night.

PHOTOGRAPHS:
ROLF BRUNSENDORF / JÖRG ZIMMERMANN

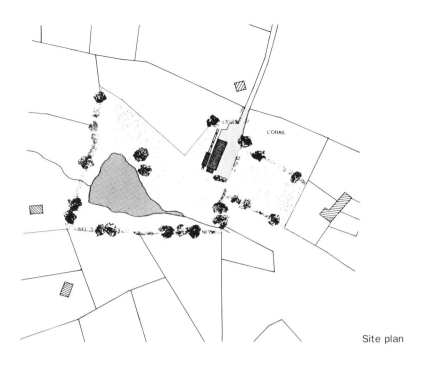

Site plan

On the opposite page we can see a view of the east facade. Their appearance has been left practically intact because most of the interventions were concentrated on the opposite facade.

Ground floor plan

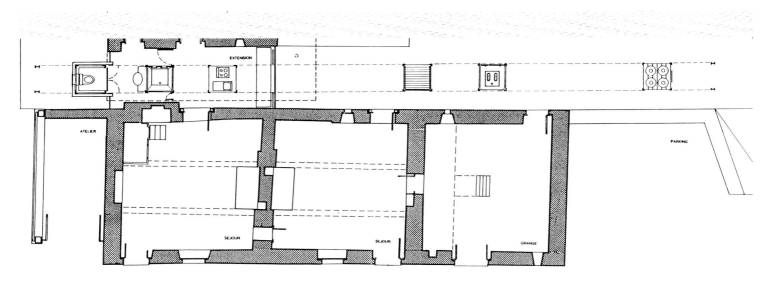

First floor plan

West elevation

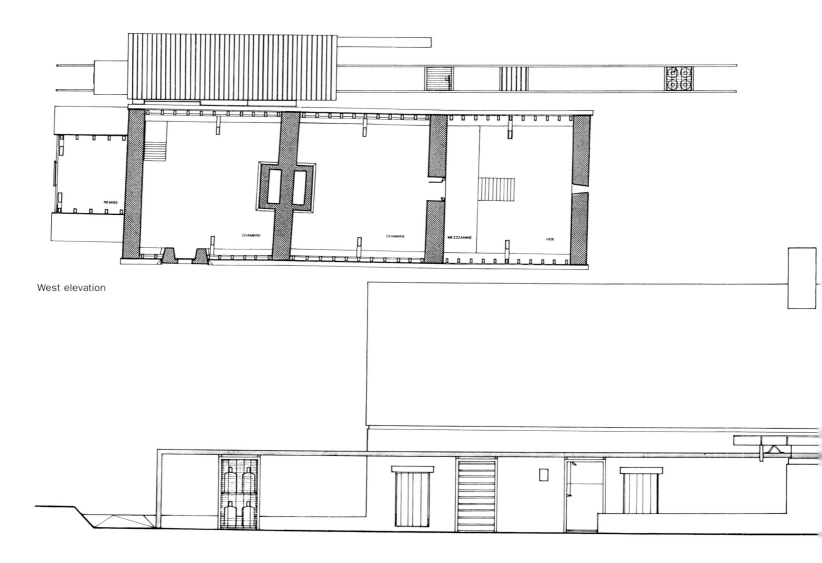

The rehabilitation carried out in this building seeks to maintain the original architectural elements and to reconstruct the defective parts using traditional materials. The annex to the original building is clearly differentiated thanks to its forms, materials and colours. This extension houses all the necessary services for making the dwelling more comfortable.

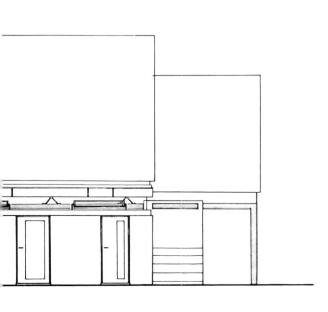

Cross-section

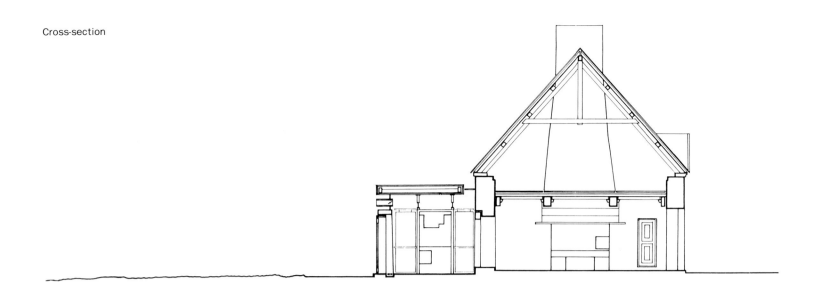

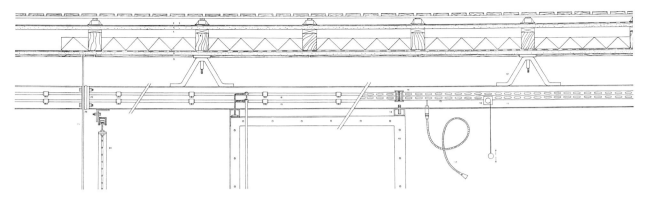

A metal structure suspended from the roof provides structural supports for the grill from which the installations and sanitary units are suspended.

Jordi BORRÀS
Carmen PADROSA

Vivenda
A CASTELLÓ D'EMPÚRIES
(Castelló d'Empúries, Spain)

This mansion located in the old centre of Castelló d'Empúries is over a hundred years old. It has a spacious ground floor with Catalan vaults of stone and brick, and a large garden of 2,300 sq m with three palm trees and a lime tree over 18 metres high. Both the building and the garden are listed and protected by the Special Plan of the old centre.

The action focused on restoring the lower and upper floors, and connecting the different floors by locating a lift in an adjoining court, outside the volume of the building. As a result, the building now houses a firm of architects and a spacious dwelling for the architects.

The characteristics of the building: on the exterior, the openings of the facade giving onto the street and the structural typology with three bays were respected.

The transverse perforation of the walls allowed a new reading of the resulting spaces, thus creating a new interplay of transparencies.

The floor was treated as a unifying element, with stone, wood and sets of carpets, and the ceilings were treated as differentiating elements of the spaces, serving as a basis for the design and allowing the other elements to be treated as furniture.

PHOTOGRAPHS:
LLUÍS SANS / CARMEN PADROSA

The space that houses the architects' office is located on the ground floor. In order to separate the working zones, a large reception room was designed with a lift providing direct access to the dwelling.

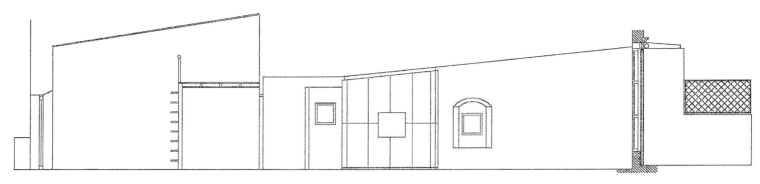

Section AA'

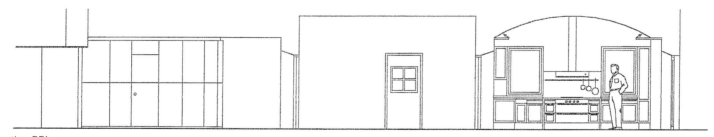

Section BB'

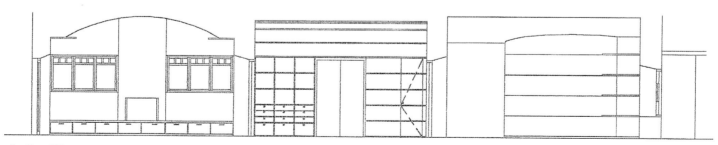

Section CC'

0   1   5

Though the outside of the building has conserved its original configuration, the interior has incorporated modern elements as part of the furniture. This combination of old and new is one of the key elements of the scheme.

The main floor features a coffered ceiling with a height of 4,5 sq m and the main living area with gold leaf paintings.

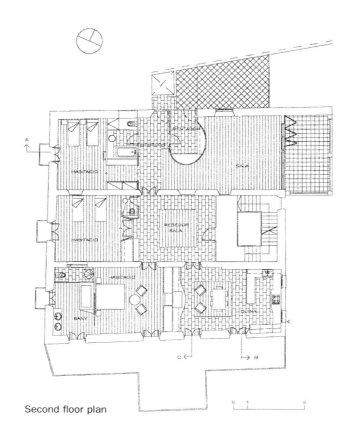

Second floor plan

OTTORINO BERSELLI & CECILIA CASSINA

Ristrutturazione IN MANERBIO
(Brescia, Italy)

The house is set at the end of a closed alley inside the urban fabric of Manerbio. It had long been uninhabited and used exclusively for storing material and equipment by a local building firm.

The poor condition of the building and the inappropriate intervention on part of the portico in the sixties did not curb the imagination of the new owners, helped and stimulated by the considerable dimensions of the courtyard and the garden.

The fascinating volumes and the need for a clear solution to the disastrous intervention of the sixties suggested the idea of proposing a sequence of very recognisable architectural elements on both the facades. The original brickwork of the portico was revealed, the stone wall was cleaned and the wooden roof structure was rebuilt.

The three-storey house of the early 20th century was recovered with the typical structure of the epoch, a stone staircase leading to the different levels and dividing each floor into two rooms.

The central body from the sixties acts as an element of union and dates the intervention.

On the facade of the extremely rational cube, the evidence of the sequence of the pillars of the portico suggested the openings, which at night-time turn the interior spaces into a permeable and transparent box.

The organic nature of the materials and the almost obsessive repetition of a single colour (floors, masonry, frames) conflict strongly with the wing of the laundry and kitchen in blood red and with the wall and the pillar of the living-room in exposed brickwork.

PHOTOGRAPHS: ALBERTO PIOVANO

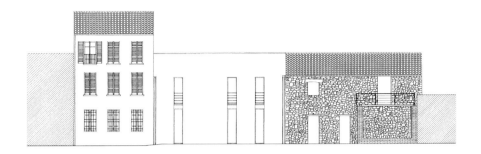

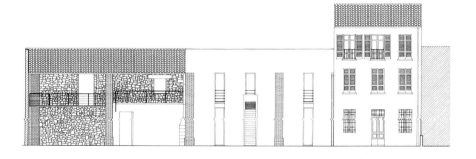

In the external appearance of the building, the project promotes verticality and linearity through the proliferation of narrow openings, thus counteracting the horizontality of the tectonic walls.

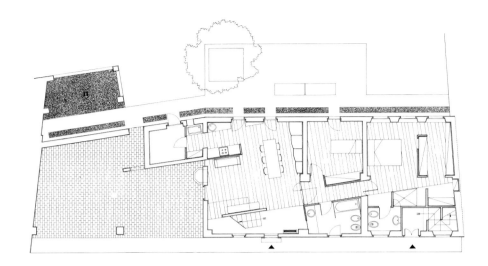

Ground floor plan

Views of the kitchen area and dining-room located on the lower level. These rooms are separated from the bedrooms by means of a fitted wardrobe that has curved metal doors with a matt finish and a swivelling door.

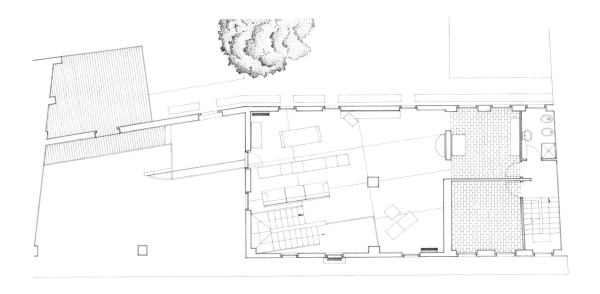

The two-flight staircase communicating the ground floor with the upper level is made of coloured, reinforced cement to which thin steel bars have been attached as a handrail.

On this page, several views of the living area located on the upper floor. This communicates with the external terrace that looks onto the garden through a small balcony and a walkway anchored to the stone wall.

DANIELE MARQUES & BRUNO ZURKIRCHEN

Haus in BERGÜN
(Luzern, Switzerland)

Marques and Zurkirchen were given a contract to cover one of the stables that are so typical of this region into two flats. The design took the old stables, a massive open structure built of piled-up stones supporting splendid roof joists, as a departure point. In this stable a wooden container was introduced.

Although the old stable has now been preserved virtually intact, the new flats look at first sight rather alien in this surrounding.

The form of the beautifully made tightly detailed the wooden box unexpectedly protrudes through the outer wall of the stable onto a narrow lane.

The stable forms the basis and the wooden container is the new element. This approach allows the two elements to blend, despite their obvious contrast. The new balconies on the front facade inserted between the old brickwork and the loggia on the roof of the wooden box also represent a direct blend of old and new. The architects have thus succeeded in making a quite remarkable building by combining the rough old stable and the refined new container. Their blending of these elements and their use of indirect references mean that the building fits in with its environment in a very subtle way.

PHOTOGRAPHS: J. IGNACIO MARTÍNEZ

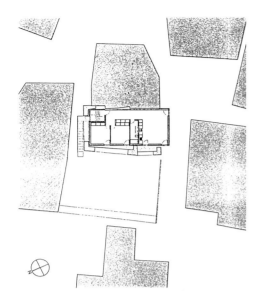

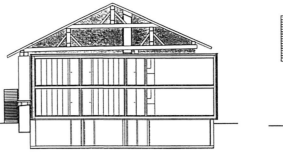

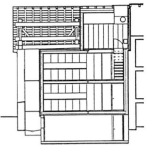

The project takes the old stable's building system as a departure point: a massive open structure built of piled-up stones supporting splendid roof joists.

At the south-west end one can clearly see the prolongation of the laminated wood container toward the exterior, contrasting with and confronting the existing stone walls. These, together with the roof, were left intact. On the right, views of the access ramp attached to the side facade.

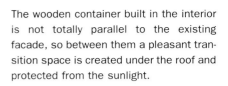

The wooden container built in the interior is not totally parallel to the existing facade, so between them a pleasant transition space is created under the roof and protected from the sunlight.

South elevation

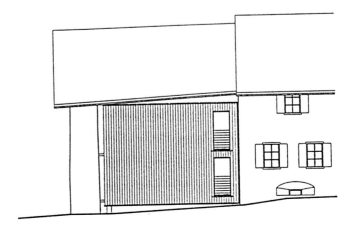

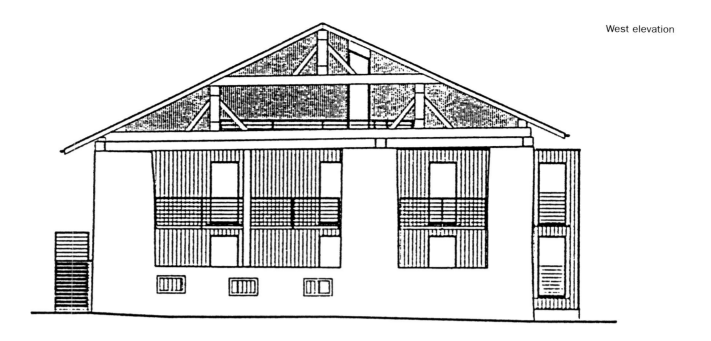

Roof floor plan

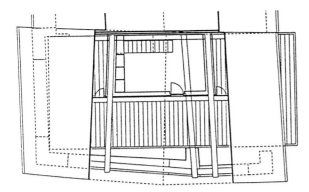

Second floor plan

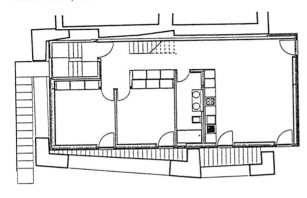

First floor plan

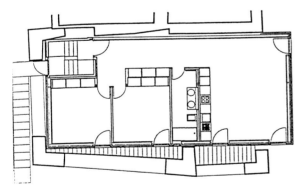

Ground floor plan

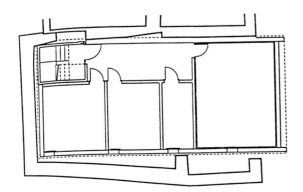

In the interior, the dwellings have been designed as totally new elements, though the structure and materials of the original building are clearly visible.

Oswald Mathias UNGERS

WASSERTURM
(Utscheid, Germany)

The original tower dating from 1957 had only the two upper floors, housing the water tank and machinery, and a high entrance hall. The kitchen floor is a new addition, and is overlooked by a gallery running parallel to the stairs. On the first level it is a newly constructed element containing the bedroom with shower, bath and fitted cupboards. The top floor is a tall space with four windows: sparsely furnished, it is a meditation area with breathtaking views over the Eifel Mountains.

As one enters to the tower one is struck by the succession of spaces that have been created: the alternation of wide-narrow and high-low. Emerging from the low, narrow stairwell there is always a high, wide space with a view of the landscape. The spaces in the water tower are simple elements stacked one on top of the other, but the art of the design lay in the adapting and refining the existent aesthetics to the new use. The spaces and materials are thus left in their purest form: sandstone, the circular form of the steps, the verticality of the layout, the new additions—all is pure, unobtrusive, natural. An example of this is that the windows largely follow the original design, serving less an idea of living space and views, and more the original purpose of illumination: one window on the stairwell, one in the kitchen and one in the bathroom. However, on the second floor the situation is different. Four windows point in the four directions, thus adding a new dimension to the circular plan thanks to the conceptual rigour of the architect, who pursued the maxim "Less is more" with laudable sensitivity.

PHOTOGRAPHS: STEFAN MÜLLER

Main facade

The down photograph shows a general view of the outside of the water tower. On the following page, view of the staircase giving access to the different levels of the dwelling.

Cross-section

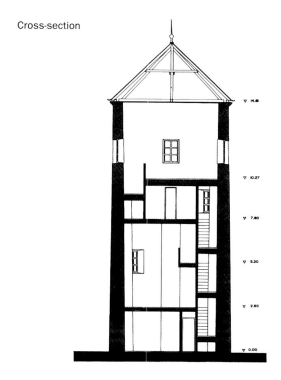

Third floor plan

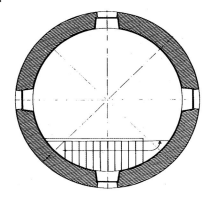

Second floor plan

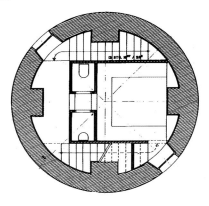

First floor plan

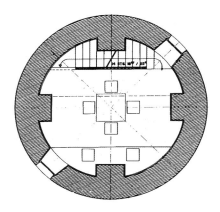

Ground floor plan

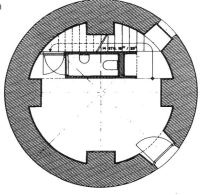

The kitchen is located on the ground floor. The down photograph shows the four interior columns that stabilise the thick sandstone walls and function as totally independent elements.

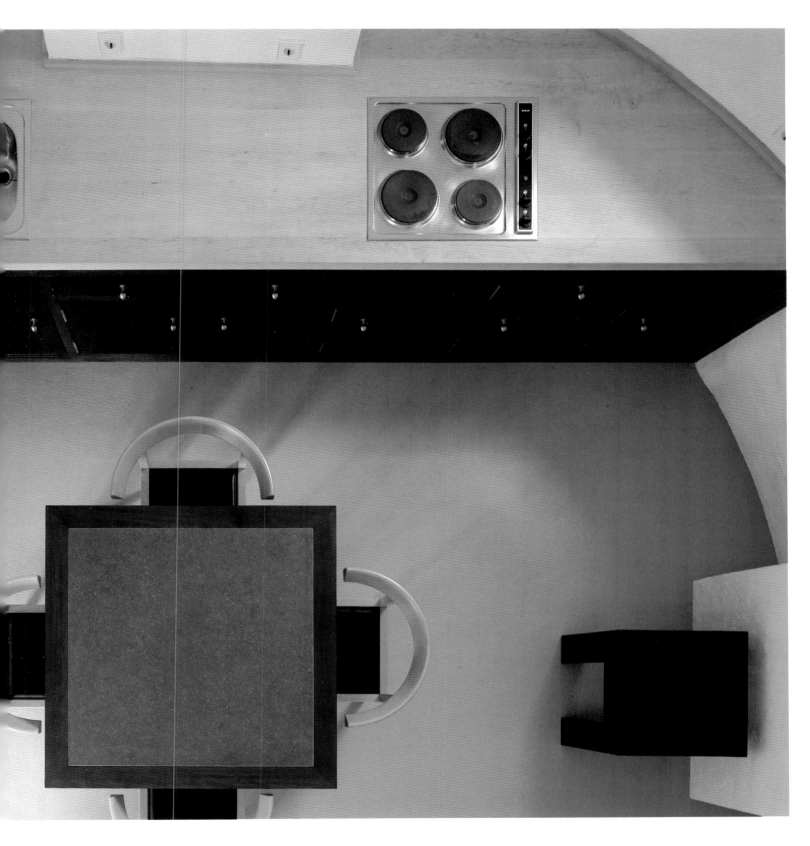

89

The project has used the existing openings except on the top floor, in which four new windows look out in the four directions.

Francesco DELOGU, Gaetano LIXI, Ricardo CONSTANTINI & Hristina ANDREEVA

Borgo DI SACROFANO
(Sacrofano, Italy)

Located a few kilometres north of Rome, the Borgo di Sacrofano is a small agricultural centre of medieval origin that sits silently in the residential fabric of the city: a disordered agglomerate of small residential units piled on top of each other, distributed around a small central square and aligned along the central street of the town. The project was to restructure on these units, located on the first floor of a building that looks directly onto the square, originally subdivided into four adjacents square parts and only illuminated on two sides with few windows. The architectural idea that guided the intervention was the desire to join the original atmospheres in a single common and continuous space, in which light plays a unifying role, an Adriane's thread that places each architectural element in connection, suggesting keys to the reading and emphasising the peculiar elements of the composition. By day, the light arrives mainly through the large skylights, while at night is regulated by means of an electric system that adapts the internal illumination to the external conditions.

A system of two orthogonal wall axes intertwines the atmospheres, cutting new volumes independent of the original walls; each element fits into the adjoining one, and forms, materials and colours come closer and move away in a sequence of elements that shapes the project by means of a single system integrated with the original structure.

PHOTOGRAPHS: ROBERTO BOSSAGLIA

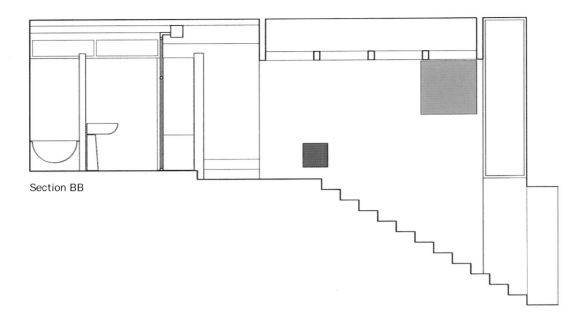

Section BB

As seen in the top photograph, the apartment looks onto a small square in the town of Sacrofano. To the right, views of the home's entrance area brought to life with coloured lights.

Ground floor plan

1. Entrance
2. Living-room
3. Kitchen
4. Office
5. Bedroom
6. Storage
7. Bathroom
8. Stairs to balcony

The apartment has been floored in stone and its walls have been stuccoed in a range of textures and colours. Furnishings are entirely in mahogany wood.

96

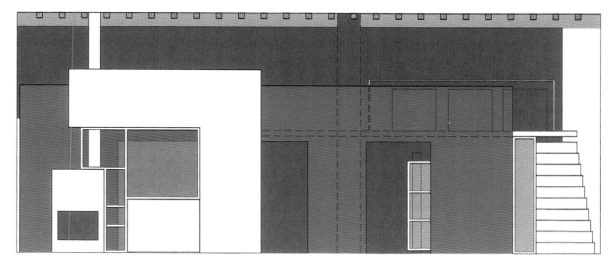

Section AA

A fluidity and permeability of space is sought through the superimposing of different planes, comprised of walls and partitions, and through the use of contrasting materials and colours. Thus, a certain theatrical sensation is created in the interior of this dwelling. Light is mostly provided by two large skylights controlled through the use of an electrical system of swivelling slats.

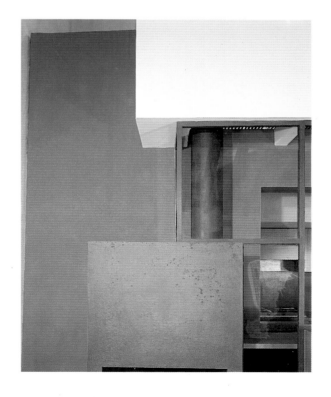

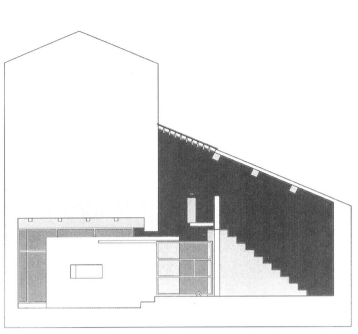

Section CC

An unfinished interior staircase leads to a small loft, housing a cosy reading area, located above the kitchen and dining-room. The new walls form a lively, many-hued chromatic range which contrasts with the original grey walls.

José Paulo
DOS SANTOS

Pousada en el CONVENTO DOS LOIOS
(Arraiolos, Portugal)

Now transformed into a luxurious hotel, the reorganisation of the different functional spaces of the convent accompanies what would be its natural expansion through time. The lower floor—almost completely dug into the earth—houses the service areas with the exception of a room to be used for conferences. The main floor houses the public areas organised around the succession of exterior spaces made up by the cloisters, patio and esplanade. The upper floor houses the bedrooms, some in the old part and remainder in the new wing.

The convent remains in its built essence very poor. Stuccoes are redone and used throughout. Stone—green xisto and granite—covers most floors. Oak is used in the flooring of bedrooms and upstairs corridor of the new wing. Local marble from unused quarries makes up the facing of bedroom bathrooms. In the interior design, done in collaboration with the architect Cristina Guedes, the oak and cherry wood furniture and other appliances have been made to measure.

Now, as before, without altering the protagonism of the existing structure—keeping all its spatial qualities intact—the addition of a new wing enclosing the eastern patio acknowledges, not only the implicit formal autonomy of the existing, but also the development of its own rules. These keep in line with the character of the materials, austere but simultaneously rich in iconography and forms.

PHOTOGRAPHS: LUIS FERREIRA ALVES

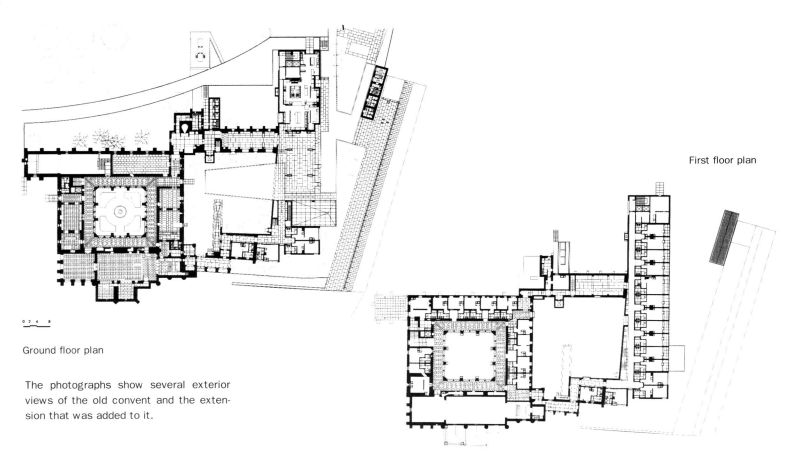

First floor plan

Ground floor plan

The photographs show several exterior views of the old convent and the extension that was added to it.

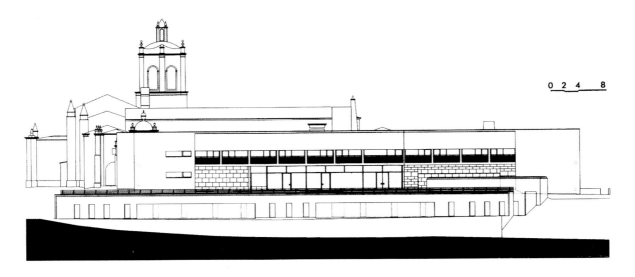

Cross-section

The public spaces of the convent, located on the first floor, are organised around a rhythmic succession of exterior and interior spaces.

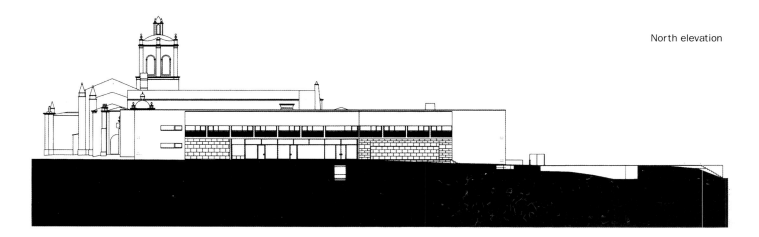

Respecting the spirit of the original building, stone remains on all the pavements except in the rooms and the corridors of the new wing, where wood was used.

Louis KLOSTER

Sola Ruin CHURCH *(Jaeren, Norway)*

The project is focused on the reconstruction of a small Romanesque church, built in open countryside near the sea. The architect wished to capture the spirit of the location, the essence of the small construction in the immensity of the surroundings.

The Romanesque church was rebuilt stone by stone, by juxtaposing the spirit of the Middle Ages and the contemporary period, it is easier to discern the contrasts in building customs and technologies, and the differing interpretations of light and dark.

The original natural dark diabase stone is used in all the walls. The joint heights in the overlaps, arches and openings have all been constructed in part based on markings and measurements from the last pre-demolition survey. To retain some of the character of the ruins the missing stone blocks are sometimes replaced by glass tiles. This also provides a deliberate articulation to the way the light is falling.

The roof construction has been recreated in the spirit of the building with massive oak timbers and inside boarding. The new floor is made in slate and conceals heating cables.

The altar is crafted from a large, rectangular stone block excavated from the foot of the tower. Lighting for the winter nights is from the simplest possible small, cylindrical pendulums.

This church used to be a closed space providing protection from the weather and natural forces, a space for contemplation and prayer. Today it is a richer space offering contact with the elements and our wider understanding of the universe.

PHOTOGRAPHS: LUI COSTA

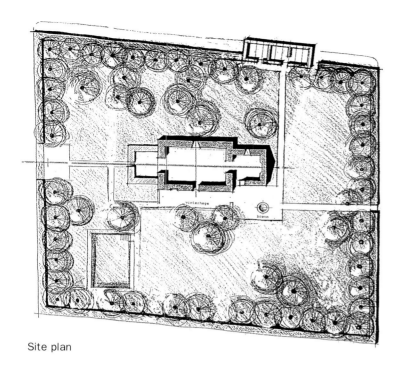

Site plan

The Romanesque church stands on a platform in the middle of a landscape dominated by the fields and the sea. During the restoration process the original stones were used wherever possible. Where they were not found, it was decided to use glass blocks, as at the top of the west facade.

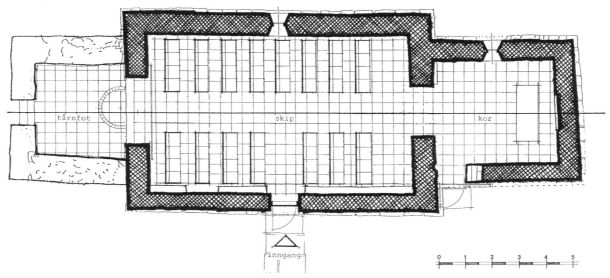

Ground floor plan

The new structure covering the building was made wih large oak boards with a continuous strip of glass forming the ridge.

Cross-section

In the places where it was not possible to find the original stones, they were replaced by glass wall faces that allow a great amout of light to enter the interior space.

Michael GRAVES

Graves Residence: THE WAREHOUSE (Princeton, USA)

The home of one of the most representative figures of postmodernist architecture, Michael Graves, is a converted warehouse, built in 1926 by Italian stone masons who built several masonry buildings at Princeton University. It was built in a typical Tuscan vernacular style using hollow clay tiles, bricks and stucco. The L-shaped building, originally divided into many storage cells, was renovated in stages. The north wing is entered through an external courtyard hat was once a lorry bay, and includes a living room, a dining-room and a long, narrow, overwhelmingly tall library with a garden terrace on the ground floor, and a master bedroom and study on the first floor. The architect retained the original concrete flooring, treating it, however, to resemble stone.

The use of daylight throughout the house deliberately reinforces the understanding of particular rooms and suggests a continuity between the building and the surrounding natural landscape. Rather than flooding the house with the diffuse light of the outdoors, Graves' more selective approach has the effect of energising the interiors with a dynamic sense of the time of day and the time of year.

The house is carefully furnished with an extensive collection of books, objects, furniture and art, creating convivial settings that convey a sense of inhabitation and reinforce the feeling of domesticity. The exterior pink stucco, the interior decoration, the niches and columns, all enhances the classical inspiration of the original building.

PHOTOGRAPHS: MAREK BULAJ

The library occupies a place of honor in the Warehouse project, facing the principal garden.
Privacy is preserved and light filtrated by the glycine of a massive pergola.

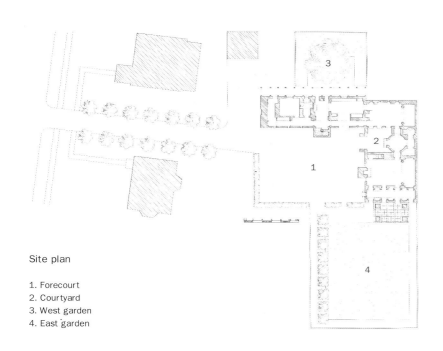

Site plan

1. Forecourt
2. Courtyard
3. West garden
4. East garden

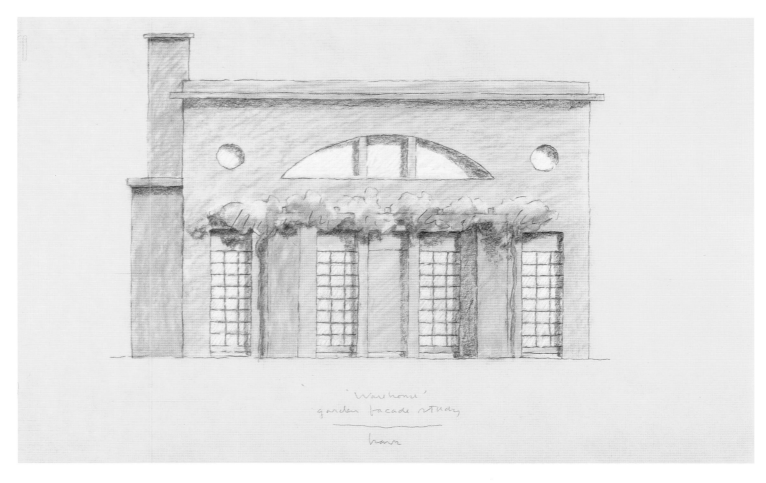

'Warehouse'
garden facade study

Ground floor plan

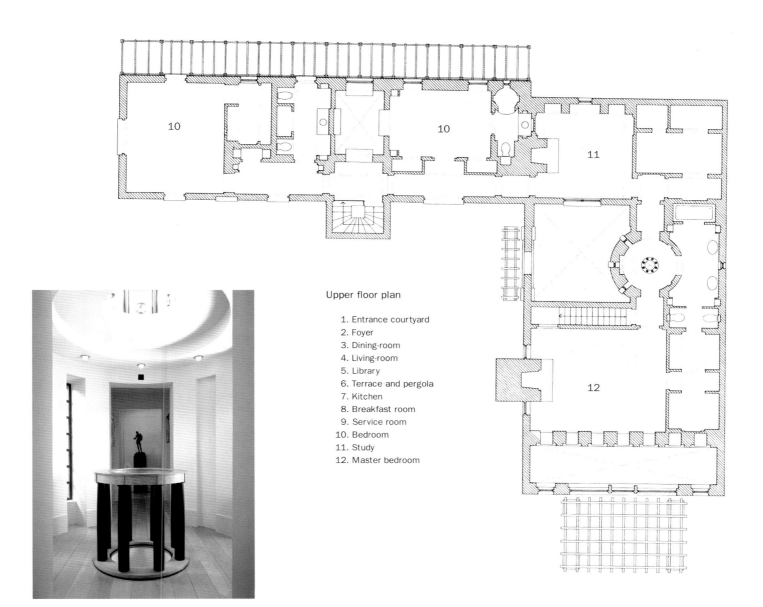

Upper floor plan

1. Entrance courtyard
2. Foyer
3. Dining-room
4. Living-room
5. Library
6. Terrace and pergola
7. Kitchen
8. Breakfast room
9. Service room
10. Bedroom
11. Study
12. Master bedroom

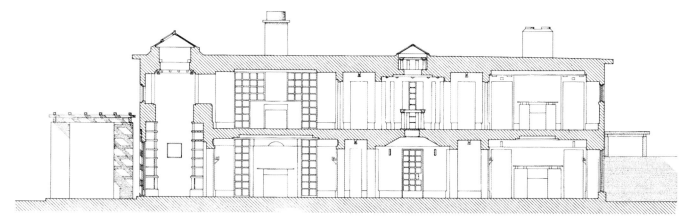

East-west elevation through north wing

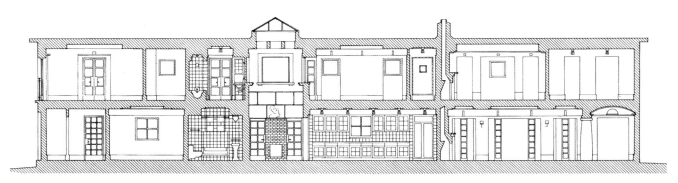

North-south elevation through west wing and north wing

North wong, section through entry, courtyard and foyer

CLAUDIO LAZZARINI & CARL PICKERING

Residence ON SICILIAN COAST (Sicilia, Italy)

In this conversion of a 19th-century villa in south-eastern Sicily into a contemporary holiday home, the client wanted a new interior—a landing with three rooms, two bathrooms and stairs overlooking a sitting room—in an existing space with double-height ceiling.

The intense Sicilian light glancing off local stone immediately imposed itself as a central theme. The villa's roof was opened to bring light into all the floors through skylights that are screened by external blinds in summer. To mark out the new windows on the elevations—loopholes landward, large ports seaward—the stone of the walls was *dematerialised* by a 300 chamfer.

Inside, the staircase is a scroll of blackened steel set in a cylindrical volume that forms a well of light, the pivot of a natural air-conditioning system that refers to Arab and Norman vernacular.

An eight-centimetre slit in the central wall of the living-room runs up eight metres to the terrace. It is toplit and throws a tracer blade of light into the room during the day, which varies its swath according to the seasons like a sundial.

Like an ode to Mediterranean light and the sea wind, this project—which was two years in the making—is a manifesto: the elegance of its honed spaces is rounded out by elaborate yet discreet details.

The villa is a concentrate of the architects' love for the stone of the south and the refined use of *poor* traditional materials.

It bears witness to their skill in inventing or reinterpreting highly functional construction systems in an artistic way.

PHOTOGRAPHS: GIOVANNA CIPPARRONE

The new openings on the exterior of the villa take the form of small narrow cracks. They are thus distinguished and are superimposed clearly on the existing openings without altering the general image of the building.

First floor plan

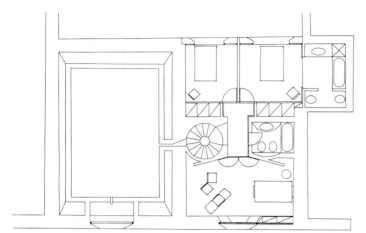

Ground floor plan

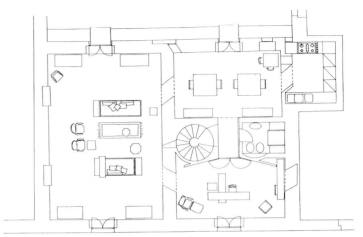

The elegance and sobriety of the interior spaces, in which the use of traditional material prevails, is compensated by small details that are elaborated and discreet. On this page, images of the crack in the central wall of the living-room.

AA Cross-section

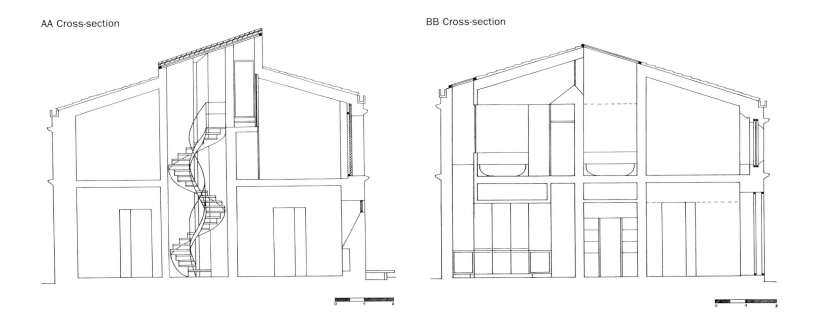

BB Cross-section

The dematerialisation of the bevelled angles, the unexpected cuts in the walls, the skylights and the angled openings create unexpected perspectives of the interior of the dwelling and allow a greater connection between rooms with minimum modifications to the original structure.

An organic spiral staircase communicates the ground floor with the upper level and the terrace, which is protected by a light glass and metal structure.

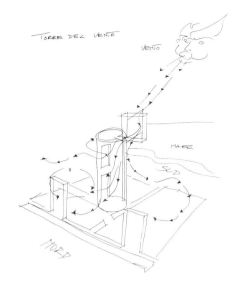

TORRE DEL VENTO

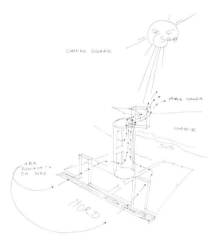

133

Alois PEITZ

St. Maximin SPORTLICHES UND KULTURELLES ZENTRUM
(Trier, Germany)

The three main requirements of the brief to restore St. Maximin church were its conversion for accommodation of sporting and cultural activities, access to the archaeological remains beneath the church and retention of the newly restored appearance of the building both internally and externally.

The main space is reached via an extension of the former vestry, in which a foyer and the ancillary spaces are located. The wood sprung floor necessary for sporting uses lends the tall, hall-like space a warm note. Wall bars and basketball nets have been fixed to the walls of the side aisles. To protect children against injury (and the structure against damage), temporary matting is fixed to the columns during sport sessions. From an overhead gantry nets can be lowered to divide the nave into separate sections without interrupting the visual continuity of the space.

The lighting concept provides bright, cool light for sporting activities and warmer light for concerts and other cultural events. Spotlights directed to mirrored surfaces produce lighting without glare. The orchestra platform in the former chancel can be extended by means of a hydraulic lifting system. Special plaster was applied between the vaulting ribs to improve the spatial acoustics.

The newly inserted elements—windows, doors, sports equipment, the gantry, the spiral staircase in the tower, and the lighting fittings—are mainly of steel. They accentuate the rigorous architectural language of the former church space and introduce comparable modern forms without seeking historicist clichés.

PHOTOGRAPHS: TRAPP, OBERDORF & PEITZ

One of the requirements of the rehabilitation programme was to provide an independent access and to organise a route through the archaeological remains in the lower part of the church.

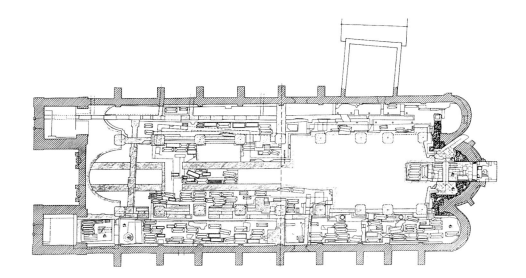

Basement floor plan

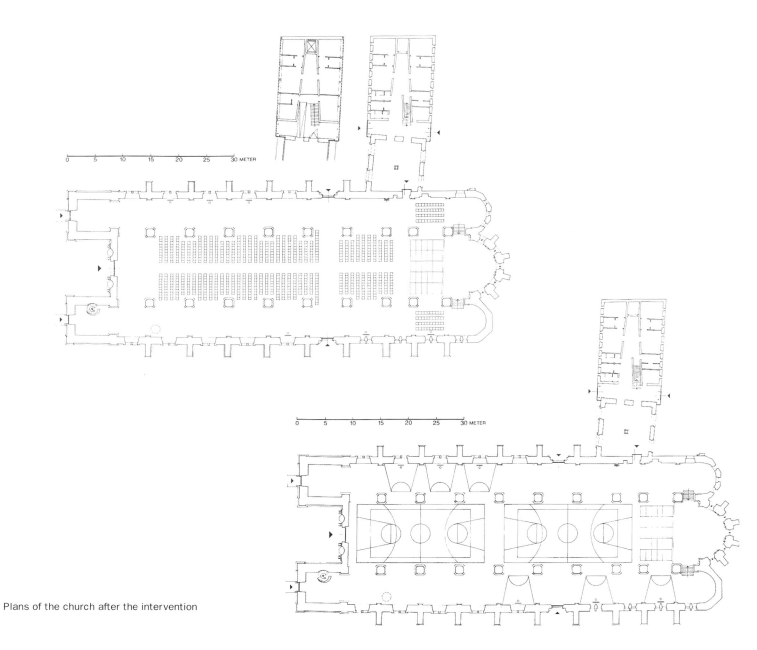

Plans of the church after the intervention

As can be seen in the photograph on the right, a system of nets descends from the upper part of the church, allowing it to be divided into different sectors without interrupting the spatial continuity.

North elevation

The top photograph shows how a system of spotlights directed to mirrored surfaces provides an even quality of lighting in the whole interior.

One of the elements added to the church is the spiral staircase that leads the visitor to the top of the tower.

Sketch

Cross-section

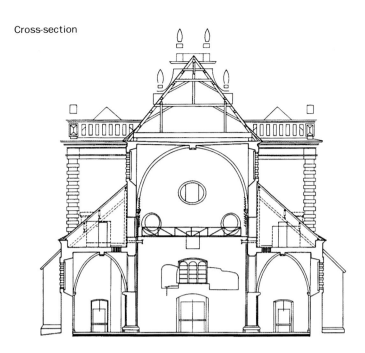

The sprung wood floor, an essential element in places used for sport, gives the church a touch of warmth.

Axonometric view

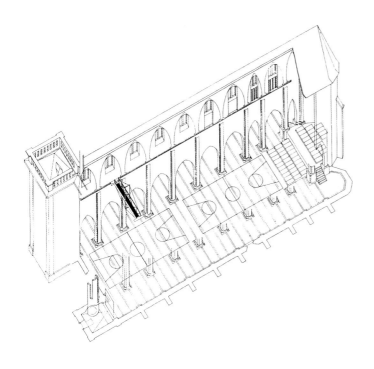

Sergio CALATRONI

Casa Galería UCHIDA (Milano, Italy)

The project consists in rehabilitating a 90 sq m space situated in the city of Milan in order to adapt it and convert it into a gallery-dwelling.

The gallery, in which works of art by the owner of the dwelling are exhibited, is on the first level. On this floor are also the kitchen and a small bathroom, whereas the upper floor is totally devoted to housing the bedroom and the main bathroom. The lower floor communicates through large french windows with a terrace that provides the space with light.

The whole project is articulated by means of fixed and mobile walls. The kitchen and the bathroom on the lower floor are separated from the gallery by means of a mobile panel. The geometric finishes of this panel were made by combining white, black and reddish wood. The floor, a magnificent surface of cherry wood, brings unity to the dwelling.

A minimalist staircase of folded sheet leads to the upper floor where the bedroom is located. The two-toned sculptural element that divides the staircase and also performs the function of a banister was made in greek-work sheet.

PHOROGRAPHS: SERGIO CALATRONI

The staircase leading to the upper floor was designed as a folded sheet.

Two views of the gallery before and after the intervention by the architect, showing the magnificent cherry-wood surface used for the floor.

First floor plan

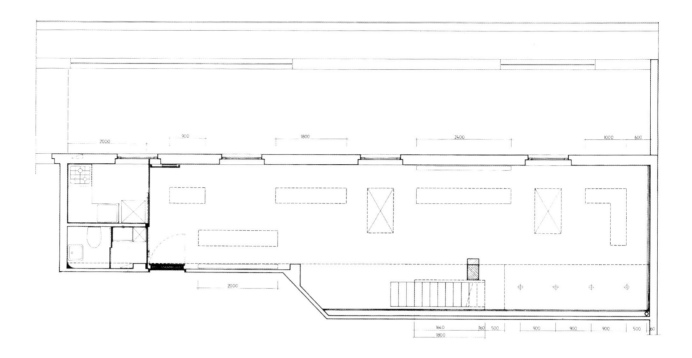

Second floor plan

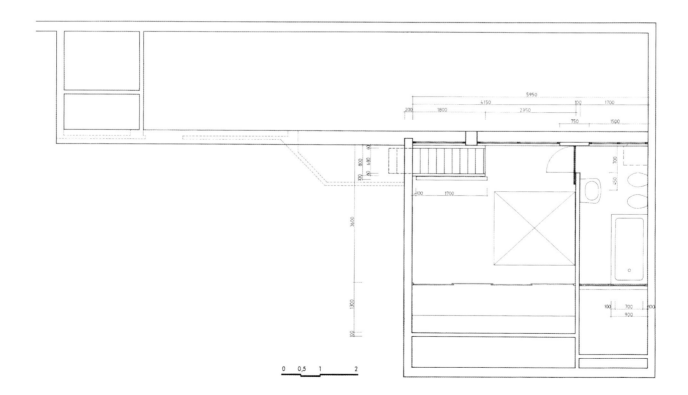

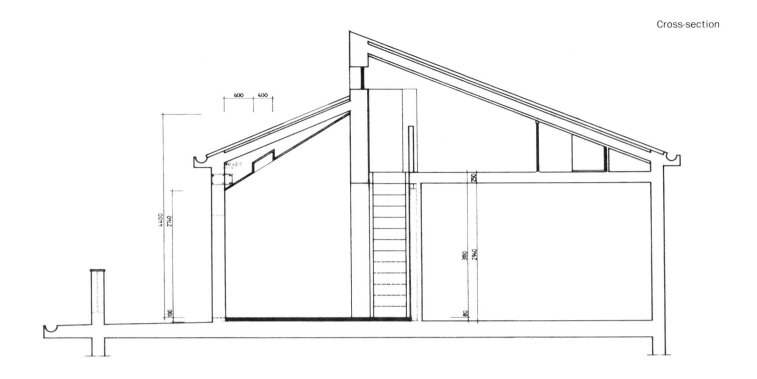

Longitudinal section of the bathroom

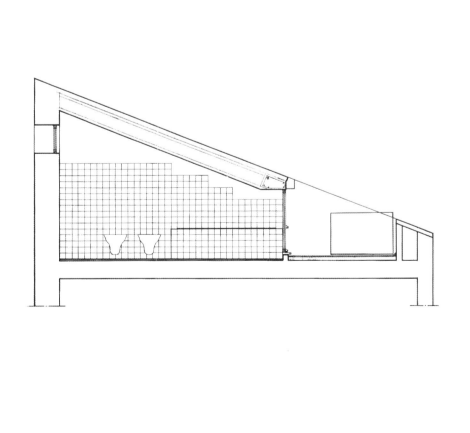

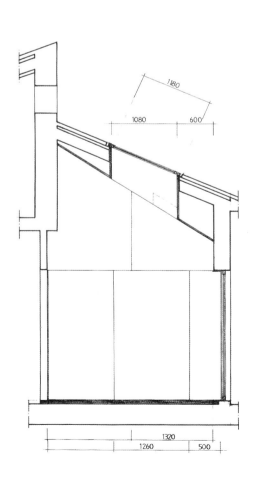

149

Longitudinal section

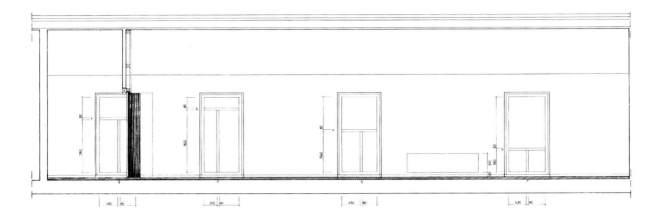

Construction detail of the window

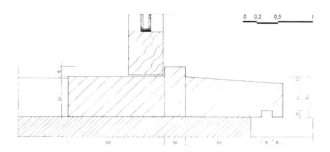

Above, initial sketch and final appearance of the mobile wall separating the kitchen and bathroom from the gallery. It combines white, black and reddish wooden panels.
On the right, a view of the area at night. The two-colour element separating the staircase is made of fretted panels.

Julia B. BOLLES
& Peter L. WILSON

HAUS DUB
(Münster, Germany)

This small addition to a 1960's Modernist atrium house respects the language of the object in which is found.

The team of architects Julia Bolles and Peter Wilson have made a careful and exquisite rehabilitation, based, as they declare, in the "fascination for clarity, optimism and simple geometries of the last days of functionalism".

The structure of the original house is transcended through the insertion of a new vertical element, a volume covered by intense blue brick that looks to the internal court. This foreign object, that emphasises and puts energy into the geometry of the complex, breaks through the artificial horizon of the existing flat roof.

Necessitated by new use requirements (a larger living space, a small studio) the new additions are reduced to five discrete elements: the blue glazed brick wall, the zinc wall, the sun louvers (a new horizontal factor), the internal swing wall and, as a nexus for the whole composition, the central fireplace.

PHOTOGRAPHS: CHRISTIAN RICHTERS

Ground floor plan

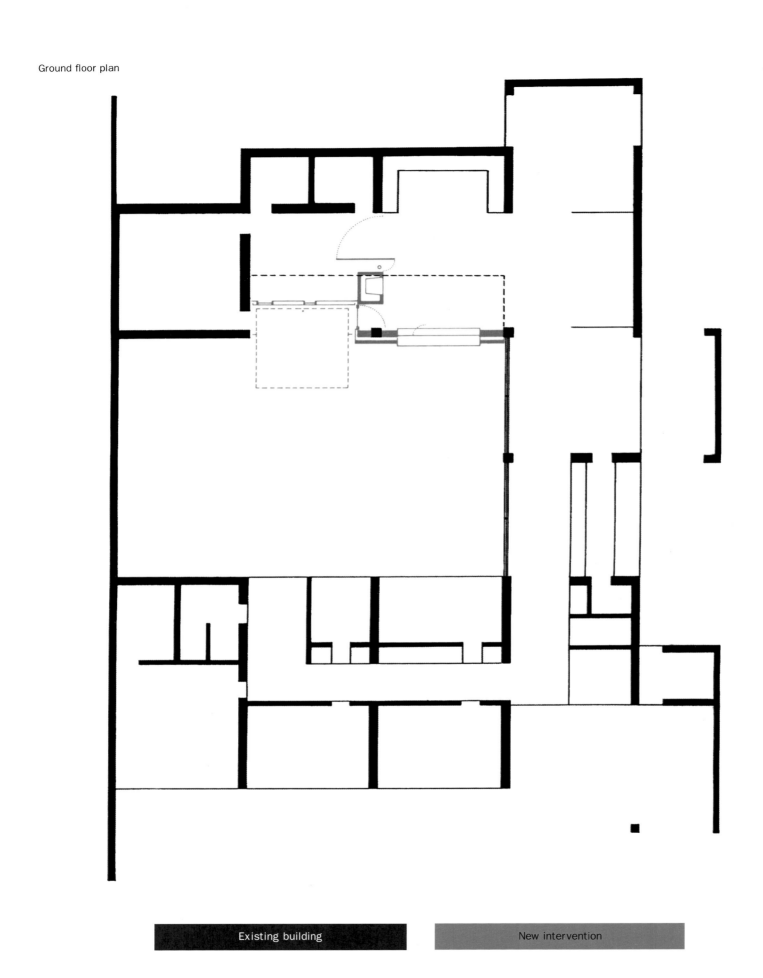

Existing building   New intervention

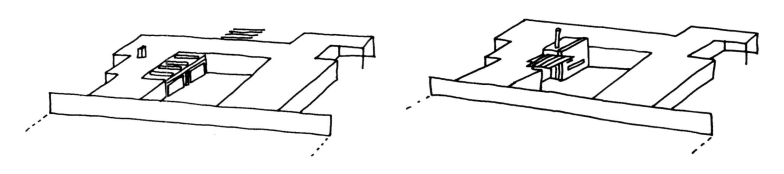

Sketches before and after the intervention

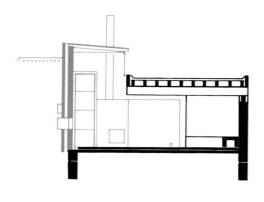

Cross-section

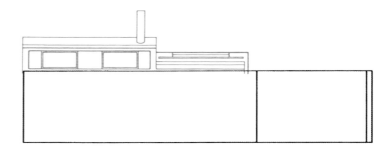

North elevation

The new fireplace, situated in a central position, acts as a link between the existing building and the elements that form the new intervention.

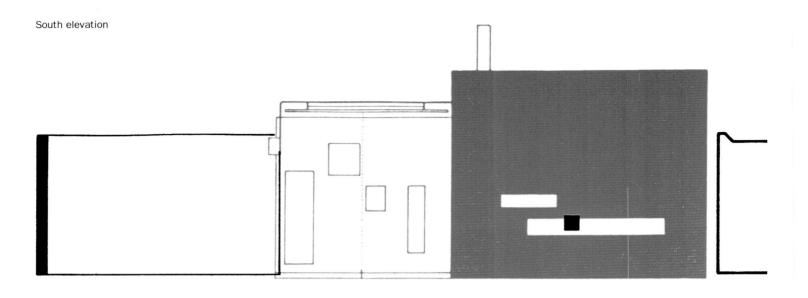

Cross-section

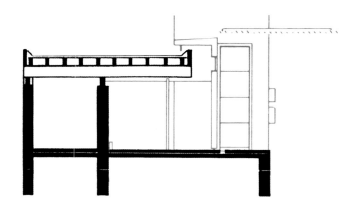

The project aims to solve the problems of space of the existing building by providing sufficient floor area to extend the living-room and create a small studio.

MATHIAS KLOTZ & FELIPE ASSADI

Hotel TERRANTAI
(San Pedro de Atacama, Chile)

The desert of Atacama is the driest in the world and it embraces 1,500x400 km approximately.

To the arrival of the Spaniards to Chile (XVI century), the Andean foothills of the north was populated by before Columbus groups whose social base was the *ayllu*.

San Pedro de Atacama was for the Spaniards, a geographical, political and social strategic point to settle down like base of conquest of Chile.

This oasis includes 20x3 km approximately. The *allyu* continues being the social base for the man, the one that is devoted to the cattle raising and the agriculture.

The Terrantai project is the recycling of an old adobe house, located in the old helmet of the town. It is in a construction context in adobe of one floor of height, continuous facade, were the public space is generated from the interior of the block. It is located to three blocks from the square and it is adjacent with the church of the town.

The responsibility consisted on building, starting from the pre-existent, 10 rooms with bathroom, dining-room, kitchen and administration offices. It was condition not to touch the adobe walls or to modify their facade, ordering the space between the walls of the place as if it was part of the town.

The project is solved starting from an internal patio of 5x5 m, around which the main dependences are generated. The rest of the program communicates with this patio by means of small stone alleys and adobe that confer to the total a village character.

PHOTOGRAPHS: ALBERTO PIOVANO

161

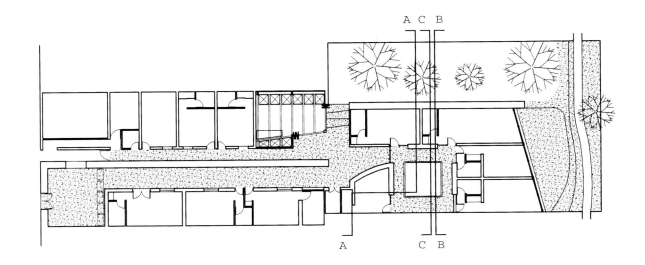

The structure of the Hotel Terrantai, located in the old town of San Pedro de Atacama, is based on the rehabilitation and reuse of an old single-storey construction, maintaining the adobe walls and the façade intact.

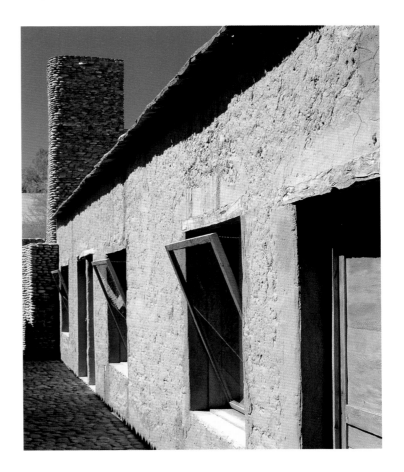

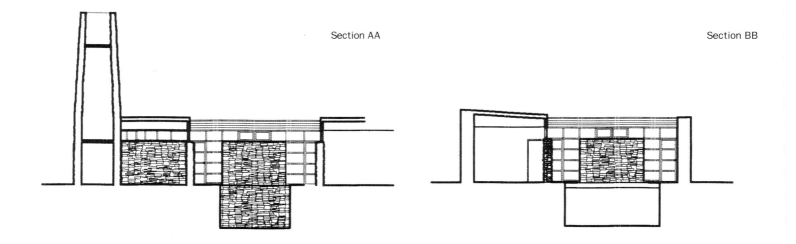

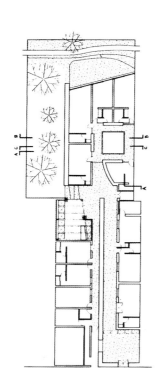

Section CC

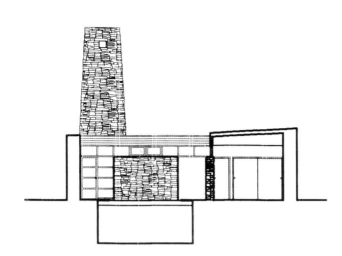

The architects emptied the interior of the site, generating a small courtyard of 25 sq m that provides sufficient natural lighting and is used to organise the spaces of the hotel on the ground floor.

The old well of the existing building generates a 9-metre-high tower that stands as the only vertical element of the group, like a large masonry chimney that establishes a certain dialogue with the steeple of the church located behind the hotel.

Pebble courses are used on some walls of the rooms and in the narrow interior streets of the building.

166

The simplicity and economy of the materials used (adobe, pebbles and wood) guarantees the integration of the project in the built environment without preventing a high degree of comfort in the ten rooms of the hotel.

The desert climate area and the local traditions caused the use of these materials. This fact led to a tectonic and introspective architecture, of closed faces and scarce windows in the thick walls.

STAN BOLT

O'Sullivan HOUSE (Salcombe, Devon. UK)

This dwelling is in a privileged setting: a strip of land framed between slope covered with thick vegetation and a small cliff that drops down to the estuary of Salcombe. Formerly the plot was no more than a strip of grasslands that belonged to the neighbouring villages. When it was put up for sale, it was subjected to a long and complex series of planning problems. Finally, the conditions of the planning permission were that the cracks in the cliff had to be repaired to stabilise and maintain the slope of the coast, and all the materials had to be transported by ship. The simple and functional design solution was conditioned by the need to respond pragmatically to these setbacks and by the desire to take advantage of the rich opportunities provided by the coastline. The desire to seek parameters such as panoramic views, light and reflections on the water led to a series of orchestrated interventions. Since the cliff required major repairs, it was stabilised by a retaining wall that extended the cliff vertically up to the height of the vaulted roof of the dwelling.

Inside this protected environment, the building was conceived as a series of introverted "boxes" that provided refuge and privacy, combined with extroverted spaces that are structured according to the demands of the inhabitants and designed to favour spatial interconnection. The abundance of glazed areas, terraces, overhanging balconies and porches that continue the perspectives are a few of the elements that helped to erode the distinction between exterior and interior. On the other hand, the sense of "refuge" was nurtured through the different private rooms.

PHOTOGRAPHS: SIMON COOKE

The combination of different construction materials such as stone and wood gives the scheme an aesthetics that is not out of tune with the environment of the estuary in which it is sited.

The roof and the volume set, that is suspended over the water, are the two architectural elements that most attract the attention at first sight.

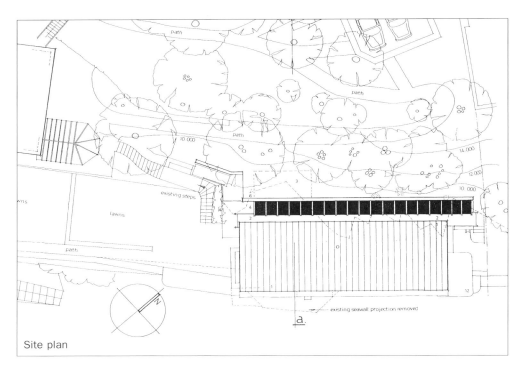

Site plan

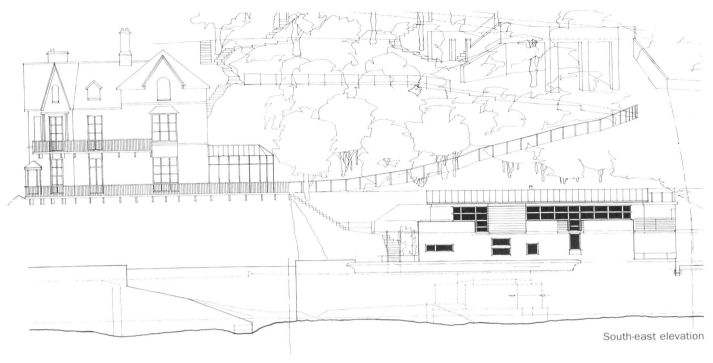

South-east elevation

173

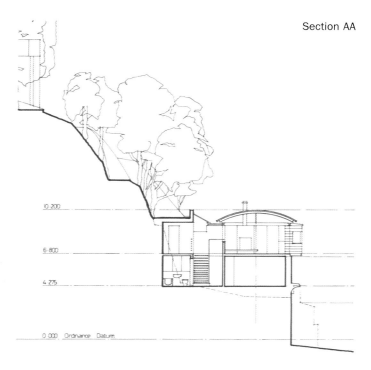

South-west elevation   North-east elevation

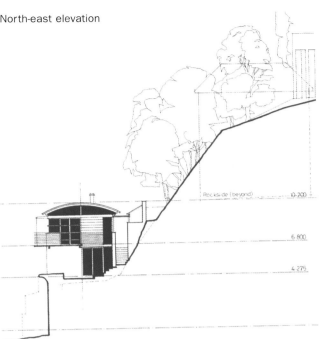

The communication between the exterior and interior spaces was a basic element in the conception of this scheme. In order to take full advantage of its privileged situation, it was decided to create a garden and to add terraces and balconies at the different ends and levels of the building.

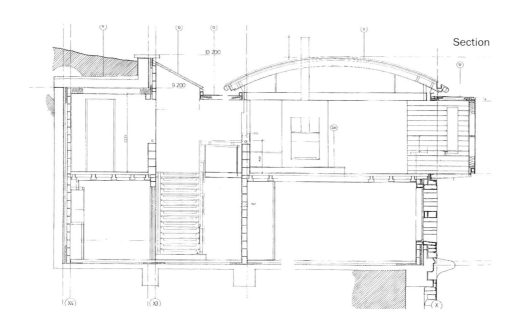

Section

177

Ground floor plan

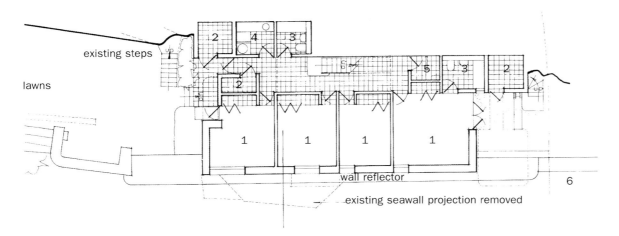

existing steps

lawns

wall reflector

existing seawall projection removed

6

1. Bedroom
2. Store
3. Bath
4. Utility
5. Shower
6. Seawall
7. Entrance terrace
8. Entrance hall
9. Void
10. Bridge
11. Kitchen
12. Terrace
13. Hearth
14. Living-dining area
15. Balcony
16. WC
17. Entrance bridge
18. Bins' store

First floor plan

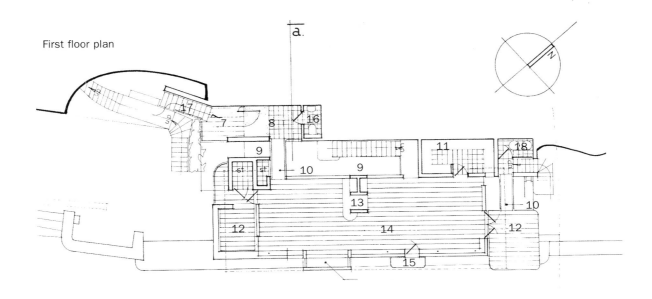

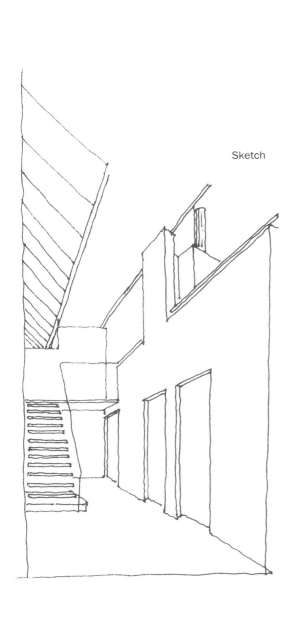

Sketch